SAVING WILDLIFE

Ocean Animals

by Sonya Newland

A⁺
Smart Apple Media

Published by Smart Apple Media
P.O. Box 3263, Mankato, Minnesota 56002

Printed in the United States of America at Corporate
Graphics, in North Mankato, Minnesota.

Published by arrangement with the
Watts Publishing Group Ltd., London.

Library of Congress Cataloging-in-Publication Data
Newland, Sonya.
  Ocean animals / by Sonya Newland.
     p. cm. -- (Saving wildlife)
  Includes index.
  Summary: "Discusses the wide array of creatures that depend on our planet's ocean ecosystems. Introduces multiple organizations
working to save endangered species of the oceans from overfishing, contamination, and global warming. Suggests ways for readers to
contribute to conservation efforts and includes maps, diagrams, and reading quiz"--Provided by publisher.
  ISBN 978-1-59920-658-5 (library binding)
  1. Wildlife conservation--Juvenile literature. 2. Marine animals--Juvenile literature. 3. Marine mammals--Juvenile literature. I. Title.
  QL82.N485 2012
  333.95'616--dc22

                                    2010039559

Produced for Franklin Watts by
White-Thomson Publishing
Series consultant: Sally Morgan
Designer: Clare Nicholas
Picture researcher: Amy Sparks

Picture Credits
Bluegreen Pictures: 9b (David Fleetham); **Corbis:** 18 (Natalie Fobes/Science Faction); **Dreamstime:** 17t (Willtu); **Ecoscene:** 16 (MC-VW); **Nature Picture Library:** 8 (Steven Kazlowski), 10b (Tom Walmsey), 26t (Conrad Maufe); **NOAA:** 9t (Florida Fish and Wildlife
Conservation Commission), 22; **Photolibrary:** Cover (Norbert Probst), 5 (Franco Banfi), 6 (Martin Harvey), 7 (Paul Kay), 15t (David B.
Fleetham), 19t (Marevision), 20b (Reinhard Dirscherl), 23t (Joe Vogan), 23b (Reinhard Dirscherl), 26b (Reinhard Dirscherl); **Shutterstock:**
10t (Four Oaks), 11 (Xavier Marchant), 12 (Ken Brown), 13b (Kirsten Wahlquist), 14t (Mana Photo), 14b (Rich Carey), 15b (Michael
Zysman), 17b (Brandelet), 19b (tonobalaguerf), 20t (Studio 37), 21t (Cigdem Cooper), 21b (tonobalaguerf), 25t (Christian Wilkinson),
25b (Richard Fitzer), 27 (Khoroshunova Olga); **Wikimedia:** 13t (Julien Willem), 24 (Dave Houston/distributed under GNU Free
Documentation License).

1019
3-2011

9 8 7 6 5 4 3 2 1

Contents

Words in **bold** are in the glossary on page 31.

The Ocean Habitat

Nearly three-quarters of the Earth's surface is covered in oceans. These huge bodies of salty water are home to some of the largest and the smallest creatures on the planet.

The World's Great Oceans

There are five main oceans. The Pacific is the largest, stretching all the way from the cold Arctic in the north to Antarctica, where it meets the Southern Ocean, the fourth-largest. The Atlantic, which is the second-largest, lies between the Americas and Africa. Next in size is the Indian Ocean, which lies to the south of Asia. The ice-covered Arctic Ocean, in the far north, is the smallest.

The Importance of Oceans

The oceans play a vital role on Earth. Air passing over the sea picks up water, which falls as rain over land. This affects **climate** and weather patterns all over the world. Beneath the oceans lie many **resources** that people use, such as **minerals** and oil. The oceans are also home to a huge variety of creatures that help sustain life on Earth.

▼ *This map shows the five main oceans, although there are many smaller seas worldwide.*

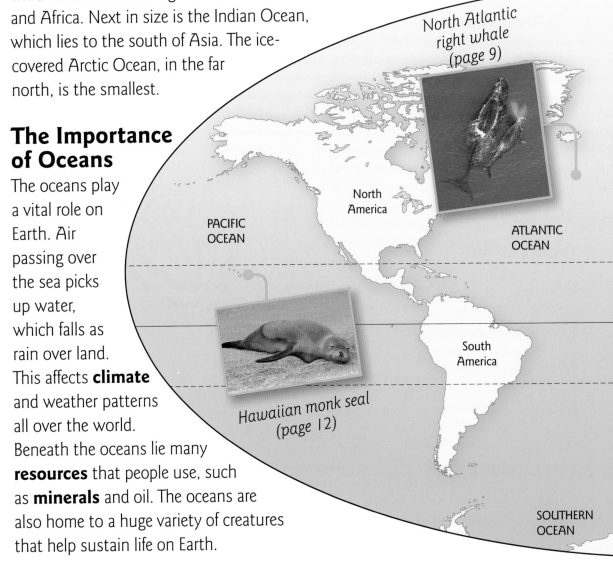

North Atlantic right whale (page 9)

North America

PACIFIC OCEAN

ATLANTIC OCEAN

South America

Hawaiian monk seal (page 12)

SOUTHERN OCEAN

Ocean Wildlife

The oceans have been teeming with creatures for millions of years. More than a quarter of a million **species** make their homes in the waters of the world. Wildlife in the water varies depending on the temperature, depth, and distance from land, but it includes everything from huge whales, such as blue and sperm whales, to **microscopic plankton**.

EXTREME ANIMALS

Sperm whales, found all over the world, have bigger heads than any other creature— about the size of a car.

66 ft. (20 m)

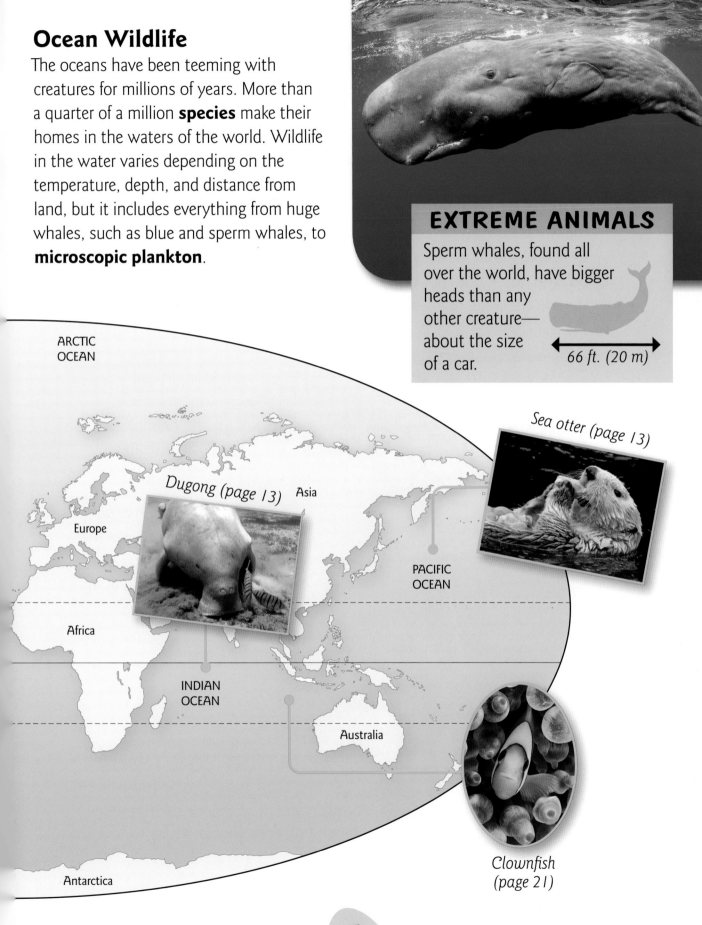

ARCTIC OCEAN

Dugong (page 13)

Asia

Europe

Africa

INDIAN OCEAN

PACIFIC OCEAN

Sea otter (page 13)

Australia

Antarctica

Clownfish (page 21)

Oceans under Threat

Some of the most unusual creatures on the planet live underwater, but the survival of many marine creatures is being threatened by humans.

Waste in the Water

The world's oceans have become a dumping ground for waste created by people. Plastic waste, such as plastic bags, is a particular problem because plastic does not break down like some other garbage, so it stays in the water for many years. Oil spills from ships **contaminate** the water and kill sea life. Another type of **pollution** is sound pollution. The noise of engines and drilling for oil underwater, for example, can disturb ocean wildlife.

◀ *This African penguin is covered in oil after a spill off the coast of South Africa.*

WHAT DO YOU THINK?

Why do you think marine creatures are important? Why should we try to save them?

ENDANGERED ANIMALS

The International Union for Conservation of Nature (IUCN, see page 28) lists animals according to how **endangered** they are.

Extinct: Has died out completely

Extinct in the wild: Only survives in captivity

Critically endangered: Extremely high risk of becoming **extinct** in the near future

Endangered: High risk of becoming extinct in the wild

Vulnerable: High risk of becoming endangered in the wild

Near threatened: Likely to become endangered in the near future

Least concern: Lowest risk of becoming endangered

Fishing for Food

For centuries, both people and animals have relied on fish as a source of food. As the fishing industry developed and more **commercial** fish were caught, numbers dropped dramatically. Now there are laws that say how many fish can be caught, but it may be too late to save some species. Other ocean creatures have come under threat because they are accidentally caught in the nets of fishing **trawlers**.

Warming Waters

Global warming is causing the oceans to heat up. Some creatures have adapted to living in cold water and may not survive as the seas warm up.

▶ *This catshark has been accidentally caught in a trawler's fishing net.*

Whales

Whales are among the largest and most impressive creatures on Earth, but some of these ocean giants may soon be extinct because of hunting and other human activities.

Whale Hunting

Throughout history, people have killed whales for their meat and the oil in their **blubber**. By the late twentieth century, many whales were critically endangered. In 1986, many countries agreed to a ban on whaling. But countries such as Japan and Norway still hunt whales for scientific and cultural reasons. Some native peoples, including the **Inuit**, are allowed to hunt whales because it is an important part of their culture and livelihoods.

▼ *Young Inuit celebrate the capture of a bowhead whale.*

WHAT DO YOU THINK?

Find out more about the arguments for and against the whaling ban. Why have some countries not agreed to it? Who do you agree with and why?

Atlantic Whales

There are only 350 North Atlantic right whales left, and this number is still dropping because many of them are hit and killed by passing ships. Despite **conservation** efforts by the North Atlantic Right Whale Consortium and other groups, it may be too late to save them.

▶ *Here, a mother North Atlantic right whale swims with her calf. The baby whales are more than 13 feet (4 m) long when they are born.*

Pacific Whales

Western gray whales of the Pacific Ocean are among the most endangered. Exploring the seas around the coast of Russia for oil has disturbed their **habitat** so badly that only 130 remain. The IUCN is working with a joint U.S. and Russian research program in the hope of saving them.

▼ *Blue whales can weigh up to 400,000 lbs (180 tonnes).*

SAVING WILDLIFE

Blue Whale

Blue whales are the largest creatures on Earth. There are fewer than 2,000 left because of pollution, whaling, and trapping in fishing nets. The Whale and Dolphin Conservation Society is one organization working to save the blue whale. Experts think numbers may be rising again slowly.

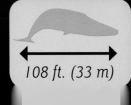

108 ft. (33 m)

Dolphins and Porpoises

Like whales, dolphins and porpoises are not preyed on by many other creatures, and not many are critically endangered. But fishing and pollution still affect these species.

Dolphins in Danger

Dolphins live in seas worldwide. They follow the same routes as tuna, so when fishing boats catch the tuna, dolphins can be caught in the nets too. You can now buy "dolphin-friendly" tuna. This is caught by using a pole and line, which keeps the dolphins safe. Dolphins are also protected by law in most areas.

◀ *As well as being caught in fishing nets, bottlenose dolphins are suffering because global warming is causing the fish they feed on to move to cooler waters.*

SAVING WILDLIFE

Maui's Dolphin
Maui's dolphins are a species of Hector's dolphin. They are the smallest and most endangered dolphin in the world. They only live off the coast of New Zealand, where around 100 survive. The New Zealand government and WWF (see page 28) have banned the use of fishing nets in these waters and have a long-term plan to save the little dolphins.

▲ *Researchers watch endangered Hector's dolphins in New Zealand. These dolphins have an unusual, rounded fin.*

EXTREME ANIMALS

The largest species of dolphin is the orca, or killer whale, which can grow up to 26 feet (8 m) long.

26 feet (8 m)

Mexican Vaquitas

The vaquita is a rare type of porpoise found in the seas around Mexico. With fewer than 300 left, these small **mammals** are critically endangered and have been named as a focal species by EDGE (see page 28). Their habitat is now a nature **reserve** to offer some protection. A conservation program has also been launched jointly by Canada, Mexico, and the United States.

Other Marine Mammals

Whales and dolphins are not the only marine mammals. Animals such as seals and otters also rely on the oceans for their food supply of fish and other sea creatures.

Saving Seals

Many seal species have come under threat because people now live in their previously undisturbed habitats. Some seals are also hunted for their fur. Among the most critically endangered are Hawaiian and Mediterranean monk seals and Galapagos fur seals. Many groups and individuals have been involved in campaigns against seal hunting. Organizations also work in seal **colonies** all over the world to save different species.

There are fewer than 1,200 Hawaiian monk seals left. They are only found on the coasts of the Hawaiian Islands in the Pacific Ocean.

WHAT DO YOU THINK?

Seal hunters say that there are plenty of some seal species, so hunting them does no harm. Other people believe seal hunting is cruel and unnecessary. Who do you agree with and why?

Dugongs

The curious creatures called dugongs live in the waters of the Pacific and Indian oceans. Across this range, many groups of dugongs are close to extinction. The largest groups can be found off the coast of northern Australia. Like whales, dugongs have long been hunted for their meat and oil, but they are also attacked and eaten by animals such as sharks and crocodiles.

▶ *Dugongs have a downturned snout to help them feed on sea grass.*

SAVING WILDLIFE

Sea Otter

Sea otters live along the coastline of the North Pacific Ocean. They have very thick fur, so they were targets for fur hunters in the past. By the start of the twentieth century, there were only around 2,000 sea otters left. A ban on hunting was introduced in 1911. Later, **reintroduction** programs bred the otters and released them back into their natural habitat.

▼ *Sea otters can twist apart shellfish with their paws to reach the flesh inside.*

Marine Reptiles

Some marine animals, such as turtles and lizards, have adapted to life in and out of the water. They can spend long periods underwater but may come onto land to breed and lay their eggs.

Sea turtles come onto beaches to lay their eggs.

Sea Turtles

There are seven species of sea turtle, and six of these are endangered or critically endangered. People have built houses and vacation resorts on their coastal **breeding grounds**, many are caught in fishing nets, and others have died from disease. Out in the oceans, turtles, such as loggerheads, mistake plastic bags for jellyfish and die when they try to eat them. WWF conservation programs set up protected areas around breeding beaches, campaign for turtle-friendly fishing, and try to stop the illegal trade in sea turtles.

There are only 8,000 hawksbill turtles left in the Atlantic and Pacific oceans.

SAVING WILDLIFE

Hawksbill Turtle

Although protected by law, many critically endangered hawksbill turtles are still caught and traded illegally. Protecting hawksbills is usually part of wider conservation programs, but in the United States there is a national recovery plan for this species. Around the world, local groups also work to protect them.

Sea Snakes

Poisonous sea snakes live in the oceans for most of their lives and most cannot move on land. Not all are endangered, but some sea snakes are **protected species**.

Marine Lizards

Other marine **reptiles** include iguanas of the Galapagos Islands in the Pacific. They are the only lizards that can live in the sea. They are considered vulnerable to extinction. All the Galapagos Islands are part of a **World Heritage Site**, which means that the animals and plants on them are protected.

EXTREME ANIMALS

The tails of yellow-lipped sea snakes look like their heads. This fools their prey into thinking they have two heads and two doses of lethal venom.

◄———————►
4.6 feet (1.4 m)

► *Marine iguanas bask on rocks to warm themselves after emerging from the sea.*

Sharks

Sharks are found in all oceans. They are the most feared creatures in the underwater world, so it might seem that little could threaten their survival. But human activity is endangering even these top ocean hunters.

Why Are Sharks Threatened?

Sharks may become caught in commercial fishing nets, but some are also deliberately hunted for food. Sharks journey to **mangrove** forests to give birth, but many mangroves have been cut down, so the sharks have nowhere to go. There are several shark species that people understand very little about, including speartooth, Borneo, and whitefin tope sharks. These may be more endangered than we know.

Basking Sharks

Basking sharks are found in oceans all over the world. These harmless sharks have been overfished for many years and are now vulnerable to extinction. They breed slowly, having babies perhaps once every four years, so if too many are killed, populations may never recover. Little is known about them, which makes conservation difficult, but several organizations are carrying out research that could help conservation efforts.

▼ *Millions of sharks are killed for their fins, which are used to make soup in Asian countries.*

16

Great White Shark

As stocks of commercial fish drop, people target more sharks for food. This could affect great white sharks, which are already listed as vulnerable. The White Shark Trust supports conservation and education programs worldwide. National organizations, such as the White Shark Research Institute in South Africa, also work to protect great whites.

▲ *The great white shark is one of the greatest ocean **predators**, feeding on fish and marine mammals.*

Philippine Whale Sharks

Whale sharks have been caught by commercial fishers for a long time. Their numbers are thought to have dropped in the past few decades, although the exact population is not known. In the Philippines in Asia, a hunting ban has been introduced, and everywhere these ocean giants live, there are local conservation campaigns.

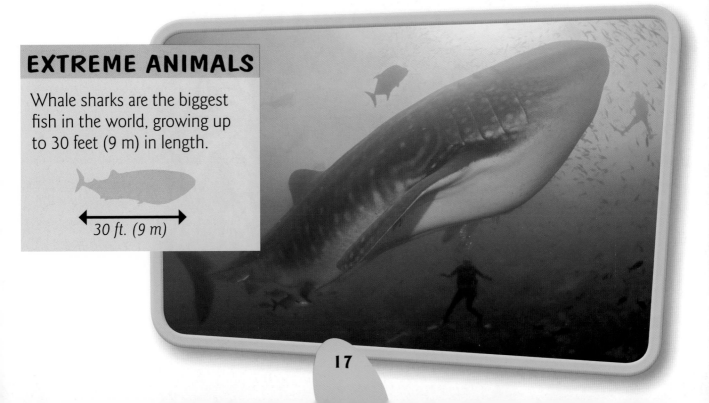

Whale sharks are the biggest fish in the world, growing up to 30 feet (9 m) in length.

←——→
30 ft. (9 m)

Commercial Fish

People have always looked to the oceans to provide them with fish for food. As fishing methods became more efficient, more and more fish were hauled from the sea. Now, some species may never recover.

Cod in the Cold Waters

A popular food fish, Atlantic cod are endangered from **overfishing**, but they have also been affected by global warming. Cod prefer colder waters, so as sea temperatures rise, they find it harder to survive. To try to reverse the damage, the amount of cod that can be caught is now strictly controlled.

WHAT DO YOU THINK?

Fishing for commercial species such as cod is often controlled by law or has been banned altogether. This might save the fish, but it affects the livelihoods of fishermen. Which is more important, human needs or those of endangered creatures, and why?

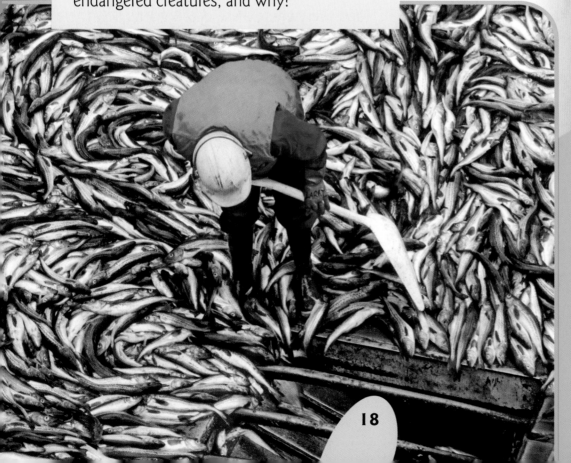

◀ Large fishing catches like this have endangered several fish species in the North Atlantic.

SAVING WILDLIFE

Bluefin Tuna

So many northern Atlantic bluefin tuna have been fished that they are now critically endangered. Many organizations have asked for a complete ban on bluefin tuna fishing, but this is not yet law. In 2009, however, the first bluefin tuna were bred in captivity, and this may help save the species.

Sturgeon

Some species of sturgeon are caught for their eggs, which are made into a luxury food called caviar. Many sturgeon are now listed by the IUCN because of overfishing and pollution. The World Sturgeon Conservation Society works to protect sturgeon and to restore populations through research and education programs. Other sought-after food fish, including swordfish, marlin, and orange roughy, are also in danger of being overfished.

▲ Marlin belong to a group of fish called "billfish." They were given this name because of their spear-like bills, which they use to stun their prey.

Tropical Sea Life

Some species in the world's warmer waters are dying out because the coral reefs on which they live are being destroyed. They are also suffering from rising sea temperatures and because so many are caught to be kept as pets.

Horses of the Sea

◀ There are around 80 species of seahorses globally. This is a longsnout.

For thousands of years, people have caught seahorses to be used in traditional Chinese medicine. As many as 20 million may be caught for this purpose every year, and this is putting populations under threat. The Seahorse Trust is one of several organizations working to preserve seahorses through research and programs such as **captive breeding**.

▲ Devil fish have spiny tails, used to defend themselves against attack.

SAVING WILDLIFE

Devil Fish
Devil fish are large rays (flat-bodied fish) found in warm waters, such as the Pacific Ocean, where pollution and accidental trapping in fishing nets have endangered them. Since the 1990s, fishing for these rays has been banned in some areas, and they receive protection in a few marine reserves around the world.

Clownfish

Clownfish live in the tropical waters of the Indian and Pacific oceans, where they have a special relationship with **sea anemones**. They eat tiny ocean creatures that could harm the anemones. In turn, the fish hide from predators in the anemones, which are poisonous to most creatures. Global warming is making the oceans more acidic, and this affects the clownfish's sense of smell, which means they cannot find the anemones. In places such as Australia, this has caused a dramatic drop in clownfish numbers.

Clownfish use sea anemones for food and shelter.

EXTREME ANIMALS

The endangered sailfish, found in warm parts of the world's oceans, is the fastest swimmer in the world, reaching speeds of up to 155 mph (250 km/h).

10 ft. (3 m)

Shellfish

Shellfish have their skeletons on the outside as a hard shell. This can put off natural predators, but it does not keep them safe from habitat loss, pollution, and being caught for food by people.

Restoring Oyster Reefs

Oysters play an important part in the marine **ecosystem**. They are a source of food for fish and sea birds. They also filter the water, removing pollutants that could harm other creatures. However, many oyster **reefs** have been destroyed as people have built homes and resorts in coastal regions. The Nature Conservancy has been working on projects to restore the reefs in countries including the United States.

▼ *Abalones have holes in their shells through which they push out water when breathing.*

Endangered Abalones

Abalones are a type of edible sea snail found in oceans around the world. Too many of some species have been caught for food, and some are now on the endangered list. In the United States, there are laws controlling abalone fishing, but more species may become endangered if they are not given protected status in other countries.

SAVING WILDLIFE

Indian Horseshoe Crab

Rare horseshoe crabs of India and Bangladesh contain a **protein** that can detect the bacteria that cause the illness meningitis. They are considered very valuable in medicine, and illegal trade is widespread. The Ecological Research and Development Group (ERDG) runs the Horseshoe Crab Conservation Fund, which gives money to local communities that work to protect the species.

▲ *The spiny tail of the common horseshoe crab is used to propel itself through the water.*

Queen Conchs

Queen conch shellfish were such a popular food in Asia and the Caribbean that by the 1980s, overfishing had caused them to become endangered. Countries including the United States have banned trade in conch meat. In the Caribbean, where many queen conchs are found, there is a program to protect the species.

▼ *Queen conchs have two eyestalks, each with a large eye at the end and a small tentacle.*

Sea Birds

Thousands of birds live along the world's coastlines and use the oceans as a source of food. Many thousands more travel across the seas every year, feeding on fish on the long journey.

Magenta Petrels

Once, the biggest danger to sea birds was hunting for their meat and eggs. Today, pollution such as oil spills and disturbance of their coastal breeding grounds are greater threats. One of the most critically endangered sea birds is the magenta petrel. There are thought to be no more than 15 breeding pairs left in the whole world, all of them on Chatham Island in New Zealand.

◀ *A conservation worker holds a rare magenta petrel in the specially protected breeding area on Chatham Island.*

Albatross

Several albatross species are under threat, mainly from pollution. They are also harmed by line fishing. They try to take the bait from the end of the fishing lines, get caught, and drown. The Agreement on the Conservation of Albatrosses and Petrels (ACAP) was established in 2004, and 13 countries are now members of this international agreement. WWF also works with national groups and governments all over the world to address the dangers facing albatrosses.

EXTREME ANIMALS

The wandering albatross has the longest recorded wingspan of any bird at 11.91 feet (3.63 m).

11.91 ft. (3.63 m)

Protecting Terns

The California least tern and the little tern are just two of several tern species under threat. Local and national organizations try to protect colonies of these sea birds. They carry out research and work especially to stop mining in areas inhabited by the birds, which disrupts their breeding patterns.

◀ *Numbers of California least terns have increased since they were given protected status in 1970.*

Weird Wildlife

The oceans are full of weird and wonderful life forms from mysterious giant squid and beautiful but deadly jellyfish to all-important corals that provide food and shelter for millions of sea creatures.

Saving Cephalopods

The group of creatures known as **cephalopods** includes octopus, squid, cuttlefish, and nautilus. These strange-looking creatures do not appear high on any endangered species lists, not because they are not under threat, but because so little is known about them. The giant squid, for example, may be endangered, but because it lives so deep in the oceans, it is difficult to know exactly how many there are.

◀ *Giant squid can reach up to 43 feet (13 m) in length.*

SAVING WILDLIFE

Nautilus

Like most cephalopods, little is known about the nautilus, but experts think their numbers may be dropping because so many are being caught to sell as souvenirs in countries such as Indonesia. Attempts have been made to breed them in captivity, but they have not been very successful. Some groups have campaigned to have the nautilus listed by CITES to stop them from being traded.

The Changing Marine Ecosystem

Corals reefs are large structures under the sea. They are made from chemicals from tiny marine creatures called corals. The reefs provide food and shelter for more than a quarter of the ocean's creatures. Corals have adapted to survive in particular temperatures, so they are affected by global warming. They are also under threat from diving tourism. Many reefs, including the Great Barrier Reef off the coast of Australia, are now protected as marine reserves.

EXTREME ANIMALS

Individual corals that make up vast coral reefs can be as tiny as just $^1/_{10}$ inch (3 mm).

▼ *A sea turtle and tropical butterfly fish swim around a coral reef in the Maldives in the Indian Ocean.*

What Can We Do?

The oceans are one of the most diverse environments on the planet and are home to some of the most important and unusual species. Today, people realize that we must try to protect ocean creatures that are endangered because of pollution, global warming, and overfishing. Local, national, and international organizations are all involved, but there are ways that everyone can help.

Find Out More . . .

WWF *(www.worldwildlife.org)*
This is the U.S. site of the largest international animal conservation organization. On this site, you can follow links to information on all kinds of endangered animals and find out what WWF is doing to save ocean wildlife.

EDGE of Existence *(www.edgeofexistence.org)*
The EDGE of Existence is a special global conservation program that focuses on saving what it calls "Evolutionary Distinct and Globally Endangered" (EDGE) species—unusual animals and plants that are under threat.

International Union for Conservation of Nature *(www.iucn.org)*
The IUCN produces the Red List, which lists all the world's known endangered species and classifies them by how threatened they are, from least concern to extinct. You can see the whole list of endangered animals on the web site as well as discover what the IUCN does to address environmental issues all over the world.

Convention on International Trade in Endangered Species *(www.cites.org)*
CITES is an international agreement between governments that aims to ensure trade in wild animal species does not threaten their survival. It lists animals that are considered to be under threat from international trading and makes laws accordingly.

U.S. Fish and Wildlife Service *(www.fws.gov)*
This government organization was set up to manage and preserve wildlife in the United States. It helps manage wildlife reserves, including those in and around seas and oceans, and makes sure laws that protect endangered animals are properly enforced.

Do More . . .

Sign a Petition

Petitions are documents asking governments or organizations to take action on something people are concerned about. Some of the organizations listed have online petitions that you can sign to show your support for their campaigns.

Adopt an Animal

For a small contribution to some conservation organizations, you get to "adopt" an animal. They will send you information about your adopted animal and keep you up to date on all the conservation efforts in the area in which it lives.

Spread the Word

Find out as much as you can about the threats to ocean wildlife and what people are doing to save them. Then tell your friends and family. The more support conservation organizations have, the more they can do!

Read More . . .

Destroying the Oceans
Protecting Our Planet
by Sarah Levete
(Crabtree Publishing, 2010)

Ocean Habitats
Exploring Habitats
by Paul Bennett
(Gareth Stevens Publishing, 2007)

Seas and Oceans
Caring for the Planet
by Neil Champion
(Smart Apple Media, 2007)

Every effort has been made by the publisher to ensure that these web sites contain no inappropriate or offensive material. However, because of the nature of the Internet, it is impossible to guarantee that the content of these sites will not be altered. We strongly advise that Internet access is supervised by a responsible adult.

Ocean Wildlife Quiz

Take this quiz to see how much you can remember about ocean wildlife. Look back through the book if you need to. The answers are on page 32.

1. How much of our planet is covered in oceans?
2. What is the largest ocean on earth?
3. Why is plastic pollution such a problem in the oceans?
4. Why did people traditionally hunt whales?
5. How many Pacific gray whales are left?
6. What has caused the drop in numbers of blue whales?
7. What is the smallest dolphin in the world?
8. Where can you find the rare vaquita?
9. Why are some seals endangered?
10. Which creatures prey on threatened dugongs?
11. Why is plastic pollution a problem for sea turtles?
12. What is the only lizard that can live in the sea?
13. What IUCN ranking is the great white shark?
14. What is the largest fish in the world?
15. In which ocean are bluefin tuna nearly extinct?
16. Why are so many seahorses caught and sold each year?
17. Which sea creatures do clownfish rely on for survival?
18. Which rare shellfish is used in medicines to treat meningitis?
19. Where is the only place in the world you can find the magenta petrel?
20. Which group of animals includes squid, octopuses, and cuttlefish?

Glossary

blubber the layer of fat beneath the skin of a whale or other marine mammal

breeding grounds areas of land or water where animals go to mate and lay their eggs or give birth to their young

captive breeding when endangered animals are specially bred in zoos or wildlife reserves so that they can then be released back into the wild

cephalopods a group of ocean animals, including octopuses, that usually have large heads and tentacles

climate the regular pattern of temperature and weather conditions in a particular area

colonies groups of animals that live and work together

commercial something that is done to make money; Commercial fishing is when fish are caught to be sold all over the world.

conservation efforts to preserve or manage habitats when they are under threat or if they have been damaged or destroyed

contaminate to poison water with solid waste or other substances, such as chemicals

ecosystem all the different types of plants and animals that live in a particular area together with the non-living parts of the environment

endangered at risk of becoming extinct

extinct when an entire species of animal dies out so that there are none left on earth

global warming the rise in average temperatures around the world as a result of human activity

habitat the place where an animal lives

Inuit a group of people native to the Arctic regions

mammals warm-blooded animals that usually give birth to live young

mangroves areas of trees and shrubs, often with their roots in the water, which grow in tropical coastal regions

microscopic something that is too small to be seen by the naked eye

minerals substances that occur naturally in the earth that people can use to make many different products

overfishing when too many of a particular type of fish are taken from the oceans so populations are unable to recover and may die out

plankton tiny plant or animal organisms that float in the sea

pollution man-made waste in the natural environment, such as chemicals in the water or gases in the air

predators animals that hunt others for food

protected species when animals are protected by law from hunting, trading, or other human activities

protein a substance found in the cells of all living things that forms hair and nails

reefs long ridges of rock, sand, or coral that lie close to the surface of the water

reintroduction when animals that have been bred in captivity are let into the wild in areas where they once naturally occurred

reptiles cold-blooded animals that lay eggs and usually have scales or plates on their skin

reserve protected area where animals can roam free and where the environment is carefully maintained for their benefit

resources things that people can use, such as oil and coal

sea anemones marine creatures that look like flowers with lots of tentacles

species a type of animal or plant

trawlers boats with large fishing nets

World Heritage Site a protected area considered to be of special natural or cultural interest

Index

Numbers in **bold** indicate pictures.

Quiz answers

1. Nearly three-quarters; 2. Pacific Ocean; 3. Plastic doesn't break down quickly so it stays in the water for years; 4. For their meat and oil; 5. 130; 6. Pollution, whaling, and accidental trapping in fishing nets; 7. Maui's dolphin; 8. The seas around Mexico; 9. Because of hunting and human settlement; 10. Sharks and crocodiles; 11. They think plastic bags are jellyfish and try to eat them; 12. Marine iguana; 13. Vulnerable; 14. Whale shark; 15. Atlantic Ocean; 16. They are used in traditional Chinese medicine; 17. Sea anemones; 18. Indian horseshoe crab; 19. Chatham Island, New Zealand; 20. Cephalopods.